THE BASICS OF BIBLICAL DISCIPLESHIP

Samson Ajetomobi

Awakening Publishing House

THE BASICS OF BIBLICAL DISCIPLESHIP
© SAMSON AJETOMOBI
ISBN: 9798598853801
Imprint: Independently published

Cover design by: Kayode Awodeji

www.menofissacharvision.com

This book is dedicated to every Christian and Christian leader who is still committed to breeding disciples according to Jesus' model.

CONTENTS

INTRODUCTION

Knowledge is power. What you know is to your advantage and what you do not know is greater than you.

The most important knowledge every Christian must seek to acquire is the knowledge of Christ – to learn of Him. Without this, it will be impossible to represent Him accurately on earth. This is what necessitated the publication of this book. Thus, our focus in this book will be an in-depth study on the principles of biblical discipleship.

Although several people are genuinely saved and truly love God with converted hearts, they do not know how to walk with Him. Therefore, we will be looking at lessons on discipleship from the biblical perspective that will guide us in following Jesus in such times denoted with perilous occurrences as we are in now.

Jesus met some young businessmen washing their nets after a frustrating period of futile toiling. After Jesus supernaturally intervened in their business, He said to them, "Follow me" (Matthew 4:18-22; Luke

5:1-11). This means that getting a breakthrough in life, or getting a miracle does not prove that you are a disciple of Jesus. Rather, it only proves that you are a beneficiary of God's power, His mercy, and His intervention. This is good to start with, but it is just a way of getting your attention to Him.

It is not having enough bread to eat or surplus raiment to put on that makes you a true disciple; it is having enough courage to follow Jesus and be what He wants you to be.

The essence of this book is to guide you to the point where you will understand what true discipleship entails; at that point, your heart would have been adequately informed to decide if to follow Jesus or just continue nominal Christianity. Eventually, you will have to make a choice. May you receive grace to choose the good path as Mary of Bethany did.

CHAPTER 1

THE SCOPE OF DISCIPLESHIP

Jesus said to them, "Come with me. I'll make a new kind of fisherman out of you. I'll show you how to catch men and women instead of perch and bass.

MATTHEW 4:19 (MSG)

During the days of Jesus on earth, fishing was a lucrative enterprise. An entire family ventured into it and even passed it on to subsequent generations. That was to show how profiting it was. Since, it was a legitimate source of livelihood, there is nothing wrong with it.

When Jesus went to the riverside to call Peter and his brother, He did not do so to render them useless for their families and the society; He went to invite them to follow another path that would make them more useful to the world at large. This path would redirect the course of their lives and guide them into the purpose of God for their lives. God's intent for you is to prosper and do well in all that you do. However, He is more interested in the prosperity of your soul. This is His intention for your life.

Jesus extended an invitation to Simon called Peter, Andrew his brother, James the son of Zebedee, and John his brother to follow Him and learn from Him how to engage in another kind of fishing – the fishing of men into the Kingdom. That invitation to FOLLOW marked the beginning of Jesus' training programme to save their souls and conscript them to save many others too. This is the crux of discipleship.

FOLLOWERSHIP IN DISCIPLESHIP

The first response in discipleship is to follow. Following Christ implies different things, one of which is that your opinion will no longer count for much because you are not the one in charge. It is your Master's opinion that matters most. Thus, to follow Christ is to surrender your opinion for His opinion.

Presently, some people are highly opinionated; they do not change their opinions easily, and they cannot be influenced easily. That is not the life of a disciple. A disciple whose heart is in the hands of the Master surrenders his opinion for the Master's opinions on all life issues. Thus, there is no argument about such vices as masturbation or homosexuality. It is the opinion of the Master that becomes his or her opinion too. No matter how much people try to play it low, he or she only sticks to the Master's opinion.

Following Jesus is a big deal. In following Christ, our opinion must be surrendered to His opinion.

Following Jesus also implies to live a controlled life. Jesus was a strange man while He was on earth because His life was controlled and planned out by His Father – His master. Everyone in His days marvelled at His disciplined lifestyle and His self-control. His entire life from the time of birth till the time of death was orchestrated by His Father. He did not come with any other personal plans. The only idea He had on how to live was all that had been spoken about Him. That was how He lived on earth. Thus, He will not train those who will follow Him otherwise.

By implication, to follow Him is to live a controlled life as opposed to being a vagrant without any guided coordination because such could make you susceptible to different kind of vices, especially from the adversary. To be called His disciple is to live a guided lifestyle, where the Master calls the shot.

The moment you start following Jesus, you cannot continue to esteem any human factor reality above biblical truth. God's word is true and can never fail. Although there are truths about life, and evidences about how we came into existence, but they do not exude the degree of credibility the word of God possesses. There is one truth that no man can alter; it is found only in God's word. When you embrace Jesus as your master and as your discipler, you embrace the truth He brings to you because He is the way, the truth and the life (John 14:6).

A practical illustration is the truth about the life of God in every child of God. Every Christian who follows Jesus should believe that the truth about the God-life in every child of God cannot be subjected to the nuances of scientific researches; it mesmerizes logical explanation. That is the same truth that becomes the prime voice over every human assertion. It cannot be understood logically; every disciple must just accept it by faith as the truth about their new life.

Every Christian must also bear in mind that to follow Jesus is to secure the path of life. There are many pathways in life; based on logic, everyone seems to know a way that seems right, but usually, the end is not always pleasant. Only Jesus can show you the path of life. On this path of life, there is the fullness of Joy. There is a path you can take where death cannot harass you, no virus can harass you, nor can any threat of life hold you down. Jesus says that He will show you that path. When you follow Him, you will secure the path of life because He knows the way.

You must know that when you begin to follow Jesus, you will not be the one in charge anymore; you must surrender self-leadership for His divine leadership. At different points in our life, we appear to know what we are doing and can discern the way we ought to go. We confidently assure ourselves that we know where we are going, but most times, we end up frustrated because we failed to see God's way for us. We must arrive at the same point Jacob arrived after he wrestled with an angel (Genesis 32:24-25); it is the point of surrendering to divine leadership.

It is fascinating how God divinely led Elisha to know the secrets of the Syrians (2 Kings 6:8-12). The King of Syria was worried and perplexed about the leak of all their strategies to his enemies. He was more disturbed about the spy lurking in their midst, taking information to his enemies. When you follow the Master, He will show you the hiding places of your enemies and all their plots. Before they ever arrive, you would have taken charge of the battle. That is the power of the man who has surrendered his followership to the Master.

When you follow Him as He demanded, you will be able to enjoy divine leadership in all areas of your life. When you follow Him, you will be able to please Him in response to His dictates in all areas of your life. This truth has been proven through diverse life experiences, and it has been certified that it pays to follow Him.

If you are choosing to be a disciple of Jesus, you must make a deliberate choice to follow Him. When He said to Peter, "Follow me", He was not deceiving him nor was He trying to force him. The supernatural encounter Peter had convinced him to follow Jesus. You might not have any supernatural encounter as Peter did, and you should not wait for one; but you must be intentional about your decision to follow Jesus.

Following Christ is an intentional and willful decision. Thus, you must intentionally surrender your will to accept His, as you admit His eternal knowledge of the encrypted pathways through the wilderness of life. You do not have to rack your brain so hard to try to decipher the path He will take you through; you just have to declare, "I will follow you." From then on, He will start taking you through a process; the process will lead you through different pathways you might not understand, just keep following, because the intention is to 'make you' as you go through those paths. At this point, your opinion will not count. Consequently, you will emerge as a Jesus' product that people in your community will come in contact with and testify that indeed you have been with Jesus.

THE MAKING OF DISCIPLES

> ***...And he saith unto them, Follow me, and I will make you fishers of men.***

MATTHEW 4:19 (KJV)

To follow Jesus is to go through a process of making. All your friends used to know you for something, but when you start to follow Him, your friends will notice a difference; they will know that something has changed about you. When you start following Jesus, transformation begins to occur within you. The Master will begin to make you to adjust and conform to His environment.

The quality of life Jesus lived and His accomplishments in three and a half years still causes uproar; He conquered the world within that short space of time. What a life!

When you follow the Master, He will make you like He was while He walked on earth. The end product of following Him is becoming like Him in all regards including exercising authority just like He did.

Peter's transformation is so fascinating. He morphed from being just a fisherman to an apostle of Christ who stood before those who mattered in his days. He was summoned before the supreme religious court of his day – the Sanhedrin, to defend his faith. He stood before that council dauntless and unapologetic about each statement he made. That council took note of him that day, and they concluded after listening and observing him critically that, indeed, he had been with Jesus. That is what it means to follow Jesus (Acts 4:1-13).

A man that says, "I have been following Jesus for ten years", or, "I have been a Christian for ten years", and there is nothing traceable to Jesus in his lifestyle is questionable. It is either that the man has not been properly discipled or someone has been deceiving him about discipleship. A man that truly follows Jesus is assured of becoming like Him. When Peter, James and John followed Him, there was a similitude of Jesus in their lifestyle and conduct. They were taken for Christ at different scenes because of their delivery capacity and their lifestyle.

To be a correct disciple believer is not to become a hermit who lives in caves, withdrawn from civilization and every social contact. That is so extreme. You should realize that the beauty of light is in gross darkness. You can reside in the same vicinity as the adversary, yet your lifestyle will not be corrupted, because Jesus has made you to become like Him – His product. The prince of this world would come to check for his stuffs in you and He will not find any, because you are Christ's product.

LEARNING OF CHRIST IN DISCIPLESHIP

To become Jesus' disciple is not a fairy tale that happens at the swing of a magic wand. To be made into the likeness of the Master, you must know that it is a process of learning. In the process of being made into His likeness, there is a life-long class you will be enrolled into; there, you will be required to learn of Him.

Take My yoke upon you and learn from

> ***Me [following Me as My disciple], for I am gentle and humble in heart, and you will find rest (renewal, blessed quiet) for your souls.***

MATTHEW 11:29 (AMP)

Learning is an exercise that requires one to adorn a studentship status. There are many things we might think we know about Christ, but when the things we claim to know are subjected to the test of time and pressure, our patience might wane. Thus, our knowledge will be futile on such occasions. There are specific classes in our learning of Christ that we must patiently attend. Failure to do so could be chaotic. Therefore, learn!

Unlike the culture of students in this age, a learner should not go into the classroom to argue with his teacher. In this age, there are a lot of arguments about how to be a Christian and how to live the Christian life. People in this age sometimes try to refute whatever instruction or correction you give them, they sometimes interpret it as condemnation. In truth, no student should go to the class to argue with the teacher because it is believed that the teacher knows something you do not know; that is why you are in class.

Jesus says, "Learn of me". In essence, He is saying that you should make Him the book you will read for you to become His product. This invitation will interrupt your pseudo-culture of being neither here nor there – just having a form of the life of Christ. You will have just one curriculum to pay attention to, which is Christ. Every other curriculum or course materials that mar the making process you are going through must be relinquished. Anytime you are learning, you also unlearn some things. Unlearn the old things and learn the new things that will make your life traceable to Christ.

This learning is in no way limited to just learning how to be a good church worker. In learning of Him, you will learn how to handle relationships, how to handle financial resources and how to deal with difficult situations of life the way Christ did. You will learn how to rebuke the fiery storms of life, how to walk in the supernatural and how to discreetly respond to the cunningness of the present-day Pharisees and Sadducees who postulate diverse theological arguments, theories and philosophies with different schools of thoughts here and there.

The greatest school of thought is the life of Christ. Learning of Him guarantees that you will become His product. His yoke is easy because it is knowledge-based. When you learn of Him, you will have a good understanding.

Understanding the Life of Christ

When the Ethiopian eunuch was returning to Ethiopia, having had a worship service in Jerusalem, Philip, being led by the Holy Spirit, ran and caught up with him to ask, "Do you understand what you read?" (Acts 8:30) That is the challenge we have with Christianity today; some people claim to be Christians but they do not understand the 'what' of Christianity, as they have not learned the man of Calvary. That is why Jesus is still asking us to learn of Him.

Today, some people are replicas of their pastors, but do not look like the man of Calvary in any way. Jesus Himself, who truly died, desired that when we learn of Him we become little *Jesus* everywhere in power, in conviction, discretion, character, and in interaction leading men to conclude that we are Jesus' product.

Learning Requires Listening

Men who learn do not argue with their instructors; they listen. Do not join the bandwagon of Christians who at every sermon feel apprehensive. Rather than adjust and let the Word save their souls, they retort, "Pastor, do not condemn me!" Nobody is aiming at condemning you. Your conscience pricks you at hearing the truth. The right response is to repent. Without listening attentively you will not be able to respond well.

You need knowledge. If you do not have the right knowledge, it is an indication that you have not learned of Him. Do not be in haste to finish the course; be patient.

Every student who goes to school attends classes and listens to the teacher, and afterwards, he or she does an examination. Before the examination period, a normal, correct, and stable student will work on what has been taught in class and use them to prepare for the examination.

In discipleship, the examinations you will take will come in forms of temptations, varying experiences, and trials as proof that you have undergone certain classes while you were learning of Him. And when you finally emerge after each level of learning, your outlook about the world around you and how you approach it will be different.

LEARN GRACEFUL COMMUNICATION

Jesus was a graceful and skilful communicator. During his public ministrations, He taught with parables, but during private moments with His disciples, He was more analytical. The moments He had with His disciples were usually quiet and private. Thus, whenever the Master beckons on His disciples to be with Him, He was inviting them to learn the unforced rhythm of grace that flows through words that quickens. Jesus shows that a man can learn to speak by grace and not by human physical forcefulness.

Having learned from the Master, you can also disarm anybody without being rough, rude, forceful, or divisive. When armed soldiers trudged into Gethsemane like they were going to war, to arrest Jesus (John 18:1-6), Jesus did not have to make plenty statements to demonstrate the degree of His power, He just said, "I am He" (John 18:6). Just that statement was enough to make those soldiers fall back.

With gracious words, you can also make your adversaries drop their weapons.

Gracious words place you steps ahead of your fiery enemies. There are words of grace that are stronger than the flames of men. When such words go out of your mouth, the impact is more than any human flames.

TAKE MY YOKE

> ***"Take My yoke upon you and learn from Me [following Me as My disciple], for I am gentle and humble in heart,"***

MATTHEW 11:29 (AMP)

Can you imagine what our world will be like if all Christians are genuinely learning Christ? Imagine if we all are learning His manner of lifestyle, His discipline, His sacrifice, His prayers, and His selflessness, there will be peace in our homes and our churches because men who have learned of Christ will not break homes or rebel against authority in their church.

Following Jesus comes with a yoke driven by Jesus. The yoke is to control our movements and curtail our ludicrous tendencies. When we take on His yoke, one of His products that will be in us is gentleness. Arrogance will leave. You will lose the capacity to perpetrate ferocious division in fellowships or gatherings of God's children. Do not become rebellious; be gentle and humble.

Gentleness

Gentleness is not that cool and calm visage you wear; it could be pretentious. When you study Christ, gentleness will just flow naturally from your heart.

If your spouse is gentle, you are blessed in your marriage. If your children are gentle, blessed is your home, as they will give you rest. If a pastor is gentle, blessed are the worshippers in such church. If you are a gentle, you are a great asset to your church. When you learn of Him, you become gentle.

Humility

A humble person serves other people. Therefore, be humble; take instructions and be teachable.

When you take His yoke upon Him, you will be teachable; you will take instructions from your pastor. You do not insist that you want to do what you like to do regardless of what anybody thinks. Insisting on what you have premeditated in your mind to do, even when someone like your pastor instructs you to do otherwise, is not the language of a man who is humble or gentle.

A humble person serves his church, his family, and at his place of work. You serve in a manner that is only traceable to a disciplined follower of Jesus. You become an asset to the Kingdom because a humble person is prone to be service-oriented.

REST: THE REWARD OF LEARNING CHRIST

A disciple who becomes gentle and humble in heart will find rest for his or her soul. Today's society is devoid of rest, as it were. On the global and national front, there is always something to be frantic about; from economic meltdown to terrorist attacks and some bizarre natural disasters. The most recent problematic issue (as at the time this book was written) that brought the whole world to a standstill is the unanticipated breakout of a deadly novel virus known as coronavirus. This virus had no regard for any status; it claimed some lives that were exposed to the disease. It resulted in terrifying unrest globally.

Deep within the soul of every man today is an agonizing yearning for rest and Jesus says that when you come to learn of Him, you will receive rest and peace for your soul. The soul of a man is made up of will, emotions, and mind. Your mind is the seat of decisions; when you do not have rest in your mind you will make poor decisions. When you do not have rest in your soul and your emotions are expressed, you will do wrong and foolish things. Some people became so extremely emotional about an issue that they responded by committing murder.

When a man finds rest for his soul, he is emotionally stable. He is sound in his mind. He does not make poor judgment about issues of life, and of cause, his energy is guardedly discharged. When you have rest and stability in the three primary compartments of your soul, you will make best decisions with your mind, you will respond to all life issues and challenges without any hassle, and your energy will be channelled to something more productive.

No man who has rest in his soul walks out of his marriage. No man who finds rest in his soul becomes rebellious and causes division and chaos. No man who has peace in his soul will start beating his wife; only a wild beast will beat his wife. Nobody who has rest in his soul will be so troubled. When you have rest in your soul, the instructions you get from learning Christ will teach your heart to stay on the Lord even when everything around you is turbulent (Isaiah 26:3). Little wonder Jesus lay quietly in the boat amid a mighty storm.

During a fiery storm, Jesus was calmly sleeping because His mind was at rest that no evil will befall Him (Matthew 8:23-24). Jesus was emotionally calm and stable because He was assured that nothing will take away what he has laboured for. *You will not lose anything you have legitimately laboured for in the name of Jesus.* Jesus' energy was well channelled. When He stood up, He rebuked the wind. He had learned to master nature.

Today, natural occurrences are the ones pushing our faith back and forth, and we are left with endless questions like, "Where is God?" "Why is this happening in our world?" Those who are raising those kinds of questions have not learned enough of Him.

When you learn of Him, He will give you instruction for a peaceful mind, and you will reach out to men.

REVIEW

- As a disciple, the first thing you need to respond to is, "Follow me".
- Jesus assures us that when we follow Him, He will make us into His likeness.
- In following Jesus as disciples, learning is very important.
- When you learn of Him you will exhibit His trait: gentleness and humility.
- He guarantees rest for your soul when you learn of Him.

CHAPTER 2

THE NATURE OF DISCIPLESHIP

> ***The disciple is not above his master: but every one that is perfect shall be as his master.***

LUKE 6:40 (KJV)

> ***A student is not greater than the teacher. But the student who works hard will become like the teacher***

LUKE 6:40 (NLT)

A disciple is a follower, learner or an apprentice. The posture of a disciple in discipleship is perpetual learning. This subjects the disciple to be under the master. Thus, a disciple is not above the master. As long as he or she keeps studying under the tutelage of the master, he or she will remain under the master. And since our master is the Lord Jesus Christ, and He is our curriculum, we are bound to be under Him and learn Him for the rest of our life and when He appears, we will be like him (1 John 3:2).

This means when we finally see Him at His second coming, there will be no doubt left in us, there will be neither fear nor questions left in us; we will be able to give answers to those doubts or questions ourselves, because our appearance will be as He is. But now, we are in the process of learning. We must never stop learning. The more we learn the more we become like Him.

Masters Influence Disciples

An apprentice doesn't lecture the master; the point is to be careful who you follow as your teacher

LUKE 6:40 (MSG)

There is a note of caution in this translation. It says we should be careful about who becomes our teacher. If your teacher, that is, the one you are following (this is not a reference to Jesus) is not following the Lord Jesus, you will likely go into error. Today, some disciples have raised other persons to follow them, but they are not passionately following the Master. The moment the person you claim to be your discipler or leader is not following the Master, his value, standard and world view will be largely influenced by other things but the Master's. There are people today who tenaciously uphold everything their discipler, leader or pastor says, even if those things are heretic. The only way to find out if your leader or pastor is teaching you truth or bunch of heresies is by diligently placing whatever he says side by side with the truth of the scripture.

Indeed, the apprentice does not lecture the master because the master knows more than him, but the point of emphasis in this text is to be careful of whom you choose to follow as your teacher. By implication, if you follow a greedy leader he will make you a greedy person; that same person will instil covetousness in you. If you follow a God-fearing leader, you will notice that you begin to tilt towards fearing God too. If you follow a leader that is humble, simple at heart and straight in his dealings, you will also become humble, simple at heart, and straight in your dealings. If you follow a very complicated person, you will also be very complicated in life, in marriage, and in everything you do. In choosing who to follow, these are a few things you should look out for:

- Does this man or woman fear God?
- Does he or she serve God passionately?
- Are his or her influences on my life and the people around him or her positive?
- Does this man or woman tremble at the word of the Lord?

Much attention should be paid to this aspect because the apex of discipleship is to become like the master. This is very critical.

Paul asked his disciples to follow him as he followed

Christ (1 Corinthians 11:1). Once a leader stops following the Master, he or she will start losing track. This should prompt you to either start praying for him, counselling with him or reaching out to him. However, do not allow bitterness or dishonour for him or her creep into your heart. Do not go about castigating your leader. Rather, honour such still and trust the Holy Spirit to guide you on the appropriate decision to make.

Besides, hearing and doing are critical in becoming like the master. Apostasy begins with not doing what you hear. At some point, you will lose your sense of direction and honour and the matter of following Jesus will be reduced to mere religion.

OBEDIENCE IN DISCIPLESHIP

Jesus learned obedience even in the process of suffering. Obedience is a core course in the school of Christ. The highest test of obedience is most apparent in the response of the flesh to instructions; there is usually a conflict between what the Master demands and our fleshly desires. Hence, we must learn how the Master subdued His fleshly desires to obey His Father. Many Christians live in disobedience because their minds desire something contrary to what God wants. Since we agreed that Jesus is our standard, one of the things we can learn from His life is that He was obedient. His was a humble and teachable life.

Today, too many Christians have the challenge of being teachable. Any scripture that is not supporting their lifestyles is taken as the perspective or view of the preacher. Now, there is no view a disciple claims to have that should not be subjected to the view of the Master. He is our highest standard. Therefore, as a follower and a disciple of the Lord Jesus Christ, we must submit our ideologies and philosophies to Christ's in obedience to Him.

DUAL NATURE IN DISCIPLESHIP

During His walk on earth, Jesus exhibited a dual nature that is figuratively represented with two different animals, the lion and the lamb whose nature typifies those natures found in Jesus. The lion nature typifies power and authority.

After His first teaching on the mountain, his listeners testified that Jesus' teaching was distinct and uniquely different from the scribes' because He taught with so much authority and boldness (Matthew 7:29). Jesus went about healing everyone oppressed of the devil (Acts 10:38). He performed lots of miracles and did lots of supernatural things that shut the mouth of His critics. That is power!

When you follow Jesus, you will realize that He was an embodiment of power. He was not a coward. By implication, anyone that decides to follow Jesus as His disciple should not ignore the power nature of the Master, else, they would miss one of the essential lessons in following the Master. We should be as bold as He was. Jesus was not fearful; He was bold. Christianity should not make you weak. You should not become easily harassed by people because you are a Christian. The fact that you are a Christian does not make you a weakling. The man of Calvary, who is your model, is as bold as a lion.

Some genuine Christian brothers and sisters are fearful; they are easy targets for harassment and intimidation at their places of work. They are not daring in any sense. You should be daring and not hold back when you ought to boldly air your view.

Peter boldly asked the Sanhedrin council to judge if it was right to obey the Master or to follow the charge of the council (Acts 4:19). It was a rhetorical way of posing to the council what they have resolved to do: never to stop preaching. The council ordered that they should be beaten and the disciples agreed to this, but they did not lose their courage and boldness before an earthly council.

The *Lion* character makes you aggressive against the camp of the enemies. David testified that when a lion and a bear showed up to steal a sheep from his flock he went after them and killed them (1 Samuel 17:34-36). That is the daring nature of the Lion of the tribe of Judah; there is no loss around Him.

You need a fighting spirit to fight your way and to

make a notable difference. Do not let others steal your position, and you say, "Well, God knows they are going to take it." NO! God only sees a coward son that cannot emulate his master. Some Christians just accept defeat under the guise of being gentle. That is not what it means to be gentle. Being gentle is not to keep quiet when being cheated and exploited; you must have the lion's nature.

While the first character is that of a lion, the second character is typical of the nature of a lamb.

Behold the Lamb of God that takes away the sin of the world
JOHN 1:29 KJV

Every disciple must have the features of a lamb.

A lamb is highly relational. Jesus did not discriminate against any class of people; He was open in His interaction with virtually everyone He met with. Likewise, a disciple of Jesus must be highly relational. You must be relational with your brethren, your family, your spouse, your children, and even sinners. As regards your relations with sinners, desist from the habit of just arriving at conclusions about them in your mind, even before ever speaking to them. You should not condemn anyone because Jesus, your Master, does not condemn even when one is caught in the very act (John 8:10-11). Rather, be non-judgmental and generous in relating with them because that was how God loved the whole world so much that He gave up Himself as an eternal sacrifice for sin, even while we were yet sinners (Romans 5:8). You should not do otherwise to anyone around you still living in sin.

A lamb is easily led. Lambs do not behave like goats, which are stubborn. When you drag a goat from a thing, it goes back to the same thing. We must not live as goats in the house of God. A goat does not heed to the pastor's instruction. A goat seems to have its mind about what he wants to do, and he does not care whosoever likes it or not. The nature of a goat is that he easily rebels. That is not the nature of a disciple; a disciple surrenders his mind.

A lamb is teachable and forgives easily. The character of the lamb reflects faithfulness either under strict supervision or without one. You cannot find a believer with a lamb's nature gossiping or tearing down another person. A lamb does not have that kind of strength; it just stays under the watch of the shepherd. A goat does not stay under the watch of a shepherd. When a goat's leg is broken, it starts returning home lamenting, "This church has no love, they did not ask about me..." However, when the goat left its covering, the pastor was not informed.

Some Christians have unguided anger. When they get angry, it is like the whole world is going to come down. That is not a healthy life of a disciple. You must be able to trust God to conquer anger. Some have all strange kinds of quest: strange attitude and lifestyle, and these lifestyles are not even traceable to Jesus. If a man will be a true disciple of Jesus he must come to a point where he follows the Master verbatim. In the course of this followership, trust the Master to deal with those strange characters in your life that does not reflect Him.

EXPRESSING THE DUAL CHARACTER OF JESUS IN DISCIPLESHIP

In relating with the brethren and your family, you should live like a lamb. Every follower should be relational and touchable. You can always relate and feel safe with a lamb. However, the lion's character is for defence and protection. It is to become aggressive at the camp of the enemy. Therefore, every believer should have this dual character and know when to exhibit either.

Do not be a lion at home; you will devour your family. Do not be a lion in the church; you will scatter the church. The church is for sheep and lambs; it is not for wolves. Thus, if a man joins a church as a wolf, the teaching of the word of God should guide his conversion to becoming a lamb and a sheep that is easily led.

You are a lion, not in your household, but the camp of the enemy. Whenever your adversary attempts to steal anything that is yours, roar back at him like a lion.

Your spouse and children should be able to relate with you. Do not turn yourself into a lion at home such that whenever your household senses your presence, they scamper for safety. People who behave like that are hypocritical; they assume a lion's character at home but are lambs on the street. That is cowardice. You should be a lamb at home and be a lion outside your home to defend your territory.

SACRIFICIAL LOVE IN DISCIPLESHIP

> ***If any man come to me, and hate not his father, and mother, and wife, and children, and brethren, and sisters, yea, and his own life also, he cannot be my disciple.***

LUKE 14:26 (KJV)

At first glance, this scripture resonate negativism because of the word 'hate'.

> ***Anyone who comes to me but refuses to let go of father, mother, spouse, children, brothers, sisters – yes, even one's own self! - can't be my disciple.***

LUKE 14:26 (MSG)

> ***If you want to be my follower you must love me more than your own father and mother, wives and children, brothers and sisters yet more than your own lives otherwise you cannot be my disciple.***

LUKE 14:26(NLT)

The core message of this text is the revelation of the love dimension in discipleship. Love, as we know it, is in levels and of diverse dimensions. This verse is making an emphatic statement about the requirement for discipleship, which is spelt out: IF YOU ARE GOING TO BE JESUS' DISCIPLE INDEED, YOU MUST LOVE HIM ABOVE ALL OTHER THINGS.

An analytical study of the list of persons in that verse reveals something fascinating. Jesus is asking you to love him more than your father. The Hebrew word for 'father' is 'source'. Our fathers are our source. They have laboured over us and raised us to where we are. We cannot deny them as our fathers. We must love and take good care of them and we must value their positions over our lives, especially when considering all that they go through. But the moment your love for your father starts conflicting with the love for Jesus in your heart, you will have to decide to follow the Lord. Your love for your father will remain, but your love for Jesus must supersede it.

Jesus is also asking you to love him more than your mother. It is very expedient that you love your mother. Mothers sacrifice so much to be sure that their children are well, become mighty, and have a great place in life. We should show our mothers great love at every level of our life. We should show them love and commitment. But when that love begins to conflict with our love for Jesus, we have to review and say Jesus is our benchmark for life.

We will love our fathers, love our mothers but not at the expense of following Jesus. Little wonder the sons of Zebedee washed their net and walked off their father (Matthew 4:21-220). They bid him goodbye to follow the Master.

Disciples must love Jesus above every other human institution. Every good husband will love his wife and every great wife will love her husband. It is so important that we love our spouses and be passionate about them; be focused and be committed to them. However, as important as that is, when it begins to conflict with our allegiance to the Lord Jesus Christ, it becomes very important to draw the line because Jesus is the benchmark.

Now, above it all, Jesus added your own life to the list. It is good for you to value your life, invest in your life, be great in your chosen career, but when your pursuit begins to conflict with your allegiance to Jesus, you need to begin to draw the line.

However, here is an important truth you should know. If you truly love God, you will love your wife, you will love your husband, and you will love your father and your mother. Once you begin to love Him on the highest note, loving people will become easier for you because God Himself is love.

Therefore, if you claim to be a disciple and want to follow Jesus, love becomes a priority.

LOVE COMPELS SERVICE IN DISCIPLESHIP

Love is that compelling act of obedience that makes you do something to someone because you just value that person greatly. To love Christ is to value Him above all human institution including your life. He becomes the topmost priority of your life. Hence, you will live a lifestyle that will not offend Him and be sold out to Him.

The beauty of following Christ based on love is that it is not out of compulsion. All your sacrifices in serving the Lord Jesus will be as an act of love, not of human reaction.

You must learn to respond to the love of God. Love makes sacrifices while following the Master without asking for human benefits. It is strange today that a supposed disciple of Jesus refuses to use his skill to serve the Master, simply because he is waiting to be paid. That is a hireling and not a disciple.

A disciple invests all his skills and life just to show his love for the Master and to advance His cause. If you are a skilful driver and there is a need for a driver in the church, volunteer your skill without asking how much you will be paid. If you are a skilful IT guru, offer your skill without asking how much you will be paid. It is so disturbing today to see men and women who are desperately monetizing their skills. It is good to monetize your skills when dealing with fellow human beings in a normal business but when

God is involved, offer your skills willingly because of your love for Jesus.

The church may pay you, but that may deny God paying you. It is a choice you have to make. Some ask, "How about the preachers? They are preaching and they are being paid." It is expedient to note that no preacher that is following the step of the Master will serve with the condition of payment. If money comes, fine! But if it does not, it is not going to change anything because preaching is being motivated by the love of God.

Thus, it is so important for you to love God to a point where you can offer your skills and expertise to joyfully advance the cause of God without expecting anything. If anything comes out of it, fine! If not, fine! Your greatest joy is that you have been able to serve your Lord and Master with your skills and your expertise. Moreover, God rewards, and He will reward you in amazing ways (Hebrew 11:6).

Love has a compelling force. Love has a way of motivating you to go an extra mile. It will make you do something to save your marriage, children, and anything legitimate. Love will make you go the extra mile in advancing the kingdom of God. Too many times, we talk about love when we do not understand it. God Himself is love; He sacrificed Himself to die because of His everlasting love (Jeremiah 31:3).

How much can you put your life on the line because you love the brethren? How much can you put your life on the line because you love the cause of God? To what extent can you put your life on the line because you love your spouse and your children? Love is demonstrated and measured in the volume of sacrifice.

REVIEW

- A student or a disciple is not above his master
- Ensure that the leader or pastor you are following is also following the Master.
- A disciple is courageous; A disciple is obedient and under authority.
- Have healthy and productive relationships; be accessible and not swift to anger. Your love for Christ must transcend your love for others and yourself.
- Love is a force that flows from a man that loves.
- Love is revealed in the sacrifice you make.
- Love for God is the benchmark of true discipleship.

CHAPTER 3

THE DYNAMICS OF DISCIPLESHIP

Among the twelve men Jesus chose to be His disciple were fishermen, a tax collector and others of diverse training. Discipleship brings in different classes of people and all manner of profession. It has no special regard for any particular profession or career path. This was what Jesus envisioned when He instructed His disciples to go into all nations to make disciples; discipleship is for all people.

Also, discipleship is not a training that needs you to start as a ready-made material; rather, it makes you into a refined material. It is a training process that most times meets you raw and crude to refine you and make you into the likeness of the Master. The first sets of disciples were not refined as it were. They were men of questionable characters and different lifestyle. But at the end of the training, majority of them emerged as refined men.

Just begin the process regardless of how good or troubled you are as there is no intention to waste you. The goal of discipleship is to get you through a process that helps you look like the One who loved and saved you. You can be so crude at the beginning, but you cannot remain crude. That is why your first course of study in becoming a disciple is the conscious effort to sit down and be with Him.

SIT WITH THE MASTER

Being with your master is to become his or her immediate assistant. This does not mean you will engage in the same activity as your master. It is not about being given an assignment but to just be with your master.

The present church has ordained a breed of strange people into leadership. As soon as a new member is seen to be available and useful, an assignment or responsibilities is given to them. And for that hasty and unwise delegation, they and the church are damaged.

Irrespective of the anointing or talent an individual has, the first thing to do in discipleship as instituted by Jesus is to sit down and learn of Christ.

How do you serve someone you are not familiar with? How do you serve a master you do not even know what gets him angry or otherwise?

A minister of the gospel who does not like locust

beans was invited by a family for a sumptuous dinner in appreciation of his impact on their lives. The hosts desiring to please their guest prepared a very delicious stew with locust beans in it. The guest had sat at the table anticipating a sumptuous meal and a great time when the meal was served and he promptly perceived the smell of locust beans. He asked his host if there was locust bean in the stew and was given an affirmative response with glittering excitement. Unfortunately, his host's excitement, which was borne out of enthusiasm to serve and please him with what they thought, was the best meal, was met with disappointment.

There are too many garnishing we are doing for the Master today that does not excite Him because those things are not in His interest. In becoming the kind of man that can represent Him, you must settle and sit with Him to know what excites Him. *What kind of meal will draw his attention?* What kind of lifestyle will compel His presence to be with you? Too many times we offer the Master what He has not required from us, because we saw it somewhere in a book, or somebody did it and it worked.

Following the master is not practising what works elsewhere; it is practising what He wants done. Acknowledging Jesus as the hallmark of our interest entails finding out what impresses Him. Pay the price of just staying with the Master; He will be so committed to you.

For His disciples not to misrepresent Him, Jesus said to them that they are not there to preach first (Mark 3:14). Oh! People are fighting to preach today. Some others fight for pulpit appearance. They are hungry for a platform just to make an appearance on the stage even if it is to take the offering or lead the opening prayer. When they are denied that opportunity, they say, "They do not need me in this church." No, you are needed; you are still being assessed to know how much you can sit to learn. Only those who sit with Him to learn will go far for Him.

SITTING WITH HIM STRIPS YOU OF PRIDE

Luke magnified a seemingly insignificant aspect of Jesus' private activities with His disciples. It is an aspect that is rarely proclaimed on modern-day pulpits.

And it came to pass, when he was come nigh to Bethphage and Bethany, at the mount called the Mount of Olives, he sent two of his disciples, Saying, Go ye into the village over against you; in the which at your entering ye shall find a colt tied, whereon yet never man sat: loose him, and bring him hither. And if any man asks you, Why do ye loose him? Thus shall ye say unto him, Because the Lord hath need of him.

LUKE 19:29-31 (KJV)

Jesus sent His disciples on an errand – a casual job not meant for matured persons like Peter. But Peter who seemed to be older than Jesus was also with other disciples to run errands. Is that not belittling? How would you have responded if you were sent on such errand?

Pride will be dealt a mortal blow when you stay with the Master. Initially, you might describe it as humiliating and being insensitive. You might even attempt opting out of the process, but you must understand that discipleship training aims at breaking you to the point that you will have nothing left in yourself to boast of. Although it is your choice to follow Jesus, you cannot be selective in what you undergo on this path.

God is far from the proud. Thus, anyone that wants to walk closely with Him must be stripped of any shade of pride. When God wanted to raise another prophet in the place of Elijah, he chose Elisha (1 King 19:19-20). The fascinating thing about Elisha was that he was a man of great substance. He had twelve oxen which are equivalent to twelve trucks today and he had servants driving each of those oxen. Elisha had so much investment. How could such man become the servant of a prophet who sheltered with a poor widow to survive famine? By human standard, that is so humiliating. Elisha did not think like human neither did he go by human standard; he was later described as the SERVANT of Elijah that poured water in his hands.

You are mistaken to think God will regard your high ranking status when He calls you to be His disciple. The first thing the Master will touch when you sit with Him is that status you esteem so high. Depending on what the Master wants to achieve with you, He might require you to relinquish your high position. This is because He will do anything to ensure no iota of pride is left in you.

To Sit with Him is to Experience Death

Dead men have nothing to prove. Only men who are still proud and envious have points to make. For instance, envying someone else who ministers better than you is an indication that you are not dead to self yet. Envy makes you create unhealthy competition with co-workers in church. But when you begin to sit with the Master, every drive you have for unhealthy competition begins to die because following Jesus is not a competition to outshine another. It is true that we still have unhealthy competitions that stem from pride and envy in our churches today; they are abysmal indications that there are still lots of acclaimed Christians who are not dead to self yet.

You cannot offer service to God out of an envious heart. God will not accept it. Envy is toxic; pride is toxic. They corrupt your heart to imagine evil continually. This is why you need to sit with the Master. He will sit on you like a refiner of silver and gold to thoroughly purge you till you emerge as He is. Bitterness that stems from envy will be flushed out. Race to outshine another will be purged out. It is in sitting with Him that you emerge as He is.

SIT AND LEARN THE MASTER'S GOODNESS

Jesus was a good man when He walked the earth. The bible says that everywhere He went He did good things (Acts 10:38). He was a man you would love to be around always because He would do only good things to you. Churches will be good when everyone in church does good; fellowship with other brethren becomes joyful when no one is thinking of how to bring you down or mess you up or take advantage of you. This act of goodness can start with a true disciple of Christ. If a true disciple starts an act of goodness, it will communicate a message of goodness to the recipient; this could motivate the recipient to demonstrate same to another and then to another until it becomes a common thing to do good to everyone around. This cycle of goodness will create an ambience of love and goodness where no member of that church will be stranded. No one will lack bread. No one will lack good job, and because everyone in the church has the good interest of others at heart information about opportunities will keep streaming in.

SIT WITH HIM; BECOME BOLD LIKE HIM

In a previous chapter, we talked about the natures of Jesus as a lamb and a lion. As a lion, Jesus was bold. He was not cowardly. Peter, one of the disciples of Jesus, also expressed this nature having been with Jesus for over three years. During his early days in ministry, he faced fierce oppositions from the Jewish leaders as his master did. The Jewish leaders apprehended him and threatened him not to talk about Jesus anymore. Peter without mincing words boldly responded to their threat. His bold response swept the Jewish leaders off their feet. Their unanimous assessment of Peter after he responded was that his boldness could only be traced to the man of Calvary – Jesus Christ.

Now when they saw the boldness of Peter and John, and perceived that they were unlearned and ignorant men, they marvelled; and they took knowledge of them, that they had been with Jesus.

ACTS 4:13 (KJV)

As a disciple of Jesus Christ, you are not a coward. You are not fearful of anything. Every disciple who had a staying and sitting time with Jesus will become bold as He.

Nothing makes Christianity very exciting like the power of God, and no power is displayed without boldness. We need this dimension of Jesus' life to reveal God to our generation.

It is not enough to know through learning that Jesus is as bold as a lion, become as bold as a lion too.

Be bold because the Master calls you brother.

Both he that sanctifies and they who are sanctified are all of one, for which cause he is not ashamed to call them his brethren so Jesus was not ashamed to call us his brethren.

HEBREWS 2:12 (KJV)

Jesus is not ashamed to call anyone who has sat with Him and followed Him, brother. This is an amazing privilege. Peter knew this and it strengthened his convictions about his place in Jesus. He was bold before mortal men to defend his convictions. You too are in the process as Peter. And Jesus will never deny you as His brother. This assuring truth will make you bold before anyone.

The more we behold Jesus, the author and finisher of our faith, the more our level of confidence arises.

They looked unto him enlightened and their faces where not ashamed

PSALM 34:5 (KJV)

Beholding the Master is also a guarantee that you will never become dormant and irrelevant. Christians who do not behold Jesus continuously will not be lightened. This could lead to shame on earth.

Rather, engage the words of the master continually.

Let my heart be sound in thy status that I be not ashamed. Let my heart be attractive to your word that shame may be far from me

PSALM 119:80 (KJV)

Whenever your heart is drawn to His word, shame will be far from you. Nothing strengthens the heart of a man like the word he hears and engages.

WALK WITH THE MASTER

Walk with me and work with me – watch how I do it. Learn the unforced rhythms of grace. I won't lay anything heavy or ill-fitting on you.

MATTHEW 11:29 (MSG)

This translation employed two different verbs to amplify the message of that text. The first is "walk" and the second is "work". The order of usage is such that being with Jesus comes before doing anything for Him: walk then work.

When you are in a hurry to work for Him without walking with Him, you will likely serve Him what He does not require. The benefits of staying with Him are numerous, and there is a way He wants Christianity to be represented. We can only learn this if we walk closely with Him to watch Him. Do not do it the way you feel it should be done. Do not do it with your standard. Watch the way He does it. Watch His sacrifices, commitments, and dedication level. Watch His focus, strength, and watch Him at the moment He is in His weakest point.

Watch Him when it seemed He was under pressure. Watch Him when He is strong. When He appeared He was losing life battles, He told three of His disciples that His soul was vexed and troubled and He needed them to pray with Him, though they slept off. This singular experience shows how much Jesus made Himself vulnerable for men who stayed closely with Him. Jesus was not opened to men who are beneficiaries of His powers, healing, and miracles, but to His disciples who sat and walked with Him.

Every time He appeared in the crowd, He prayed and healing and deliverance occurred. People rejoiced! However, the only people that saw Him cry were His disciples who sat and walked with Him. Discipleship is at its climax when you can see the vulnerability and low moments of your master.

To be with Christ means you will see His supernatural and natural parts. What do you know about His lifestyle when He walked on earth? Apart from the heavy messages and manifestations, what have you learnt about His frailty and struggles as a man on earth?

If you are a disciple of Jesus, you will not feel too arrogant to ask brethren to pray for you because Jesus Himself asked His disciples to watch in prayers with Him. A true disciple will not arrogantly parade around as someone who knows everything there is to know and does not need anyone's help. That you have to appear strong all the time is a subtle lie! The Master brought His disciples so close to Himself and they watched and followed Him. One could only wonder what could be in the minds of the vocal Peter when Jesus requested prayers from them. Would they have taken Him serious? Yet, Jesus did that to let them know that the season He went through is the same season they will go through. He showed them how to triumph and not fail. He exemplified how they should react to various seasons of life.

Just as Jesus was tempted, you will be tempted as His disciple too. Just as Jesus was persecuted, you are will be persecuted as His disciple too. Just as Jesus was mocked, you are will be mocked as His disciple too. Just as Jesus was deserted, you are will be deserted as His disciple too. Learn more of Him until you pass the test. By the grace of God, you shall pass the test.

Be a Practicing Disciple

> ***O Theophilus, these are the report you require to know concerning Jesus, that Jesus Christ of Nazareth. This is all he began to do and to teach.***

ACTS 1:1 (KJV)

When you start working without walking, you are likely to submit an unacceptable work to the Master. That is why some works are not acceptable to God because they are done out of strange heart.

Do you teach patience and you are not patient at all? Do you teach giving and you are not a giver? It is hypocritical. Become a practitioner of what you teach. Demonstrate love and teach it.

Jesus laid down the pattern for communicating doctrines – do it before teaching it. Thus, before your next privilege to stand before a pulpit to preach, what have you been doing?

REVIEW

- Jesus chose very strange characters that were seemingly unfit for ministry as His disciples.
- To be with Jesus is to be with Him to understudy His dispositions in all life circumstances.
- To be with Him is to learn to talk the way He speaks words of grace.
- To be with Him is to learn His manners and attitude when under pressure, during surplus and scarcity.
- To be with Him is to know how to present the gospel at the risk of your life.
- Jesus taught and lived by his lifestyle. Be a

practitioner.

CHAPTER 4

THE DISCIPLINE OF DISCIPLESHIP

Discipleship is one of the most critical subjects in the body of Christ. When Jesus was leaving the earth He told His first disciples to go into the world and make disciples of all nations, which includes all tribes, every belief, every sector, every language and every group on earth (Matthew 28:19). This order is different from what most churches celebrate today – they make converts and magnify it as an achievement. To make converts is good, but it is not the ultimate.

New converts are babies that still possess tendencies to do things the Master will not approve of. However, there are disciplines that every convert should follow that will prove them as disciples of Jesus and make them conform to the life of Christ.

Jesus Christ is the core objective of discipleship. Every discipline, training and process that comes with discipleship is geared towards conformity to Jesus Christ. Hence, any other curriculum or training process in any Christian community that is not designed to transform new converts to become like the Master is null.

REGIMENTATION OF DISCIPLES

And it came to pass, when Jesus had made an end of commanding his disciples, he departed thence to teach and to preach in their cities

MATHEW 11:1(KJV)

When Jesus finished placing this charge before his twelve disciples, he went on to teach and preach in their villages.

MATHEW 11:1 (MSG)

When Jesus had finished giving instructions to His twelve disciples, He went on from there to teach and to preach in their (Galilean) cities.

MATHEW 11:1 (AMP)

And it came about that when Jesus had come to the end of giving these orders to his twelve disciples, he went away from there, teaching and preaching in their towns.

MATHEW 11:1 (BBE)

The translators of the King James Version used the word "commanding" to describe Jesus' interaction with His disciples. This word is descriptive of a military regiment. Three other translations used other words that are dominantly used in the military lexicon. This means that discipleship is military in its outlook; each word employed by the four translations quoted above will be examined to explain the disciplines involved in discipleship.

Command

A command does not leave you with rooms to make comfortable choices of what to obey or what to ignore. A military man does not think of impossibility whenever assigned a duty. The extreme cost of the duty would be his life which he has been trained to give up.

Hence, when you choose to be a disciple of Jesus, you have chosen to receive commands from the Master. It also implies that you have enlisted as a soldier at His command (2 Timothy 2:3-4).

Commands are not usually convenient; no soldier has ever received a command and begins to laugh with excitement; he just responds in the affirmative. We all indeed have many things we would love to do at our convenience, but discipleship trims down our options for convenience. Commands take out your freedom to just loiter around. It grows you into a disciplined Christian with a definite purpose for every resource at your disposal.

Commands require prompt responses. Therefore, to

agree to follow the Master is to be ready to give more prompt responses to His command. A Command does not give you the option to ask questions. It just leaves you with an option to obey. Many consider this to be too rigid and not an element within the ambit of grace. This is one of the reasons we are yet to have men like Jesus today. Jesus testified that everything you saw Him did were things He received from God (John 5:19). He had no personal agenda. That is the hallmark of a true disciple – surrendering personal agenda for the Lord's agenda.

Order

Order connotes hierarchy and structure within an organizational context. The military outfit is one of the organizations that highly esteem hierarchy and structure. No lower-ranking officer dares looks at a higher ranking officer in the eyes; it will be regarded as mutiny.

Likewise in discipleship, Jesus, the Master, is the most senior officer, and we serve His purpose on earth. Also, there are leaders in the body of Christ, who God appointed as heads and overseers to watch over us. You must be prepared to take orders from them.

Instruction

Defiance to instructions has caused a lot more havoc in different sectors of human endeavour than any natural disaster. No society whose citizens are committed to obeying instructions will be backward in growth and development.

This is not limited to the secular context; church people defy instructions, especially the ones they feel is stringent. Those are the types of people who have not sat with the Master, nor learned anything Him.

Unfortunately, many Christians are not well enlightened to know that defiance to instructions, especially the seemingly insignificant ones, comes with consequences. When the consequences come, they blame it on some other agencies. Obedience to instructions can preserve your life but every time you break an instruction, it costs you more to recuperate.

True disciples of Jesus are committed to receiving instructions from Him.

Charge

A charge is an authoritative command or instruction to do something. Just like a command, it leaves you with no room to consider options of evading the command.

There are Christians who feel they have the free will to either do whatever the Master charges them to do or ignore it. Their biased understanding of what the dispensation of grace entails makes them picky in obeying the commands of Jesus to them.

Peter and the other disciples did not question the authoritative command of Jesus; this is one of the reasons why we still talk about them today. Their obedience to those commands is our model for discipleship today.

TEST OF LOYALTY IN DISCIPLESHIP

And it came to pass, when Jesus had made an end of commanding his disciples, he departed thence to teach and to preach in their cities

MATHEW 11:1 (KJV)

There are two definite seasons during discipleship training. The first season is the season when the Master abides with the disciples. It is the season He spends time to sit with and brood on them, and ultimately imparts them with His life. The second season is usually an examination time; it is the time of departure; the Master withdraws from the disciples just for a season.

The departure of the Master for a season is to test the devotion of your heart. During this season, your heart is the hub of the test. It does not have much to do with the circumstances and situations that confront you when the Master departs; it has all to do with your heart. How will you serve when your leader or pastor is not around you for a season? How will you carry out your duties? The Master wants to test your intention for enrolling into the discipleship training.

Any Christian can sing when their emotions are high, but what happens when things fall apart? Peter was faced with one of those times just before he was arrested. Peter had vowed and boasted that he would never leave his master, he went as far as saying he would even die in His stead (John 13:37). That was daring! However, as soon as the Master was taken away to be questioned by the Sanhedrin council, and a little girl walked up to Peter querying if he was one of Jesus' followers, Peter started cursing. He denied his Master, not before armed men, but a harmless young maiden. Even with all his theatrics, Peter could not convince the young maiden that he was not Jesus' follower. He repeated the cycle of denial three times before the cock crowed. What a disciple!

Jesus had not departed for too long before Peter's devotion was tested. Three years of learning and walking with the Master seem to have gone down the drain in just a moment of test.

A student can boast to his or her teacher during classes, but during examination, the teacher will stay aloof. It is the teacher that will eventually assess the sincerity of the boastings of the student.

For everyone who claims to be a disciple, your attitude to instructions, orders and commands will be tested as soon as the Master steps aside to assess your commitment and loyalty.

Churches will be very stable and more effective with stable and consistent followers. If every Christian has a quest to be a disciple of Jesus and are ready to take command from their pastor, instructions from their leader, and respect order without trying to give excuses, there will be a total transformation in the society.

SELF-DISCIPLINE IN DISCIPLESHIP

A disciple is conditioned through continual self-discipline to be like his master. It is continuous, as chances are that once in a while you will go low or come under pressure. It is during such periods you will have to exercise continual disciplinary efforts to remain stable and focused.

Apostle Paul expressed self-discipline better with two scriptures:

> ***But I keep under my body, and bring it into subjection: lest that by any means, when I have preached to others, I myself should be a castaway.***

1 CORINTHIANS 9:27 (KJV)

> ***I know both how to be abased, and I know how to abound: every where and in all things I am instructed both to be full and to be hungry, both to abound and to suffer need.***

PHILIPPIANS 4:12 (KJV)

Only a disciplined disciple could utter such statement as Paul did.

Certain disciplines are essential for every disciple. These disciplines will keep them fit and in shape for any assignment.

THE DISCIPLINE OF PRAYER IN DISCIPLESHIP

During His days on earth, Jesus was known as a man of prayer. Prayer was His lifestyle. Jesus prayed (and still prays) without ceasing. If as a follower of Jesus you are struggling with your prayer life, your followership index will be full of queries. As students of the Master, our commitment must be to learn all that the Master did while on earth, including mastering the discipline of prayer.

Jesus had an unquenchable life of prayer. Nothing constituted a significant hindrance to stop Him from praying. He was neither stopped by the successes of His miracle-filled outreaches nor the teaching engagements nor the tedious journey from village to village and city to city. He prayed continuously.

As a disciple of Jesus, you must maintain an unquenchable life of prayer. Pray without ceasing. Pray in and out of season. Pray like breathing. Pray about everything. Never get to a point in following the Master where you ask, "Are we going to pray about this too?" Please, pray about everything.

God honours men who speak more with Him. The beauty of prayer is that the more we pray the more we look like the One we pray to. Therefore, if you want to look like Jesus, spend more time praying. You will begin to see things just from His perspective alone.

Jesus showed His disciples one of the core reasons why they must pray always – in order not to enter into temptation.

> ***And when he was at the place, he said unto them, Pray that ye enter not into temptation... And said unto them, Why sleep ye? rise and pray, lest ye enter into temptation.***

LUKE 22:40& 46 (KJV)

THE DISCIPLINE OF FASTING IN DISCIPLESHIP

> ***And when he was come into the house, his disciples asked him privately, Why could not we cast him out? And he said unto them, this kind can come forth by nothing, but by prayer and fasting.***

MARK 9:28-29

Fasting is an ancient practice of denying oneself of pleasure. Fasting is not a practice that is restricted to Christian religion only. Many other religions practice it and some even do it more than Christians. Most times people deny themselves of pleasure to go higher spiritually and advance in their life endeavours. They do it as a way of consecration to detach themselves from things that could distract them during the spiritual upgrade. Even secular businessmen do it to get fresh inspiration.

Jesus told His disciples that certain challenges will remain difficult to solve; there are mountains they will not be able to move unless they combine their prayers with fasting. Jesus' choice of words indicated that there are some challenges that you can confront and solve by just praying. But He emphasized that there are certain kinds of issues that you will need to fast before you can solve them.

Fasting is not food hunger. Fasting and prayer is a very potent weapon to subduing the oppression of the devil. It places you on a spiritual pedestal of authority where you just command and the emissaries of the devil flee.

Fasting is not convenient. It is a deliberate discipline that subdues your body and deprives it of pleasure. Every disciple who wants to do greater works on earth must give themselves to fasting from time to time. When you are faced with daunting issues, it is time to fast. When a situation is proving too difficult for you to handle, it is time to fast. Disciples do not leave anything to chance.

The disciplines of fasting and prayer are necessary for disciples to command much power on earth. These practices also afford you the privilege of fellowshipping with the Master regularly till His glory begins to rub off on you. That was the experience of Moses on Mount Sinai.

THE DISCIPLINE OF INTIMACY IN DISCIPLESHIP

Discipleship is a journey of consistent and continuous interaction with the Master, which will result in intimacy. Peter and John gave different accounts of their intimate walk with the Master after He left the earth. Peter said,

> ***For we have not followed cunningly devised fables, when we made known unto you the power and coming of our Lord Jesus Christ, but were eyewitnesses of his majesty. For he received from God the Father honour and glory, when there came such a voice to him from the excellent glory, This is my beloved Son, in whom I am well pleased. And this voice which came from heaven we heard, when we were with him in the holy mount.***

2 PETER 1:16-18 (KJV)

John's testimony of his intimacy with Jesus was close to Peter's. He said,

> ***That which was from the beginning, which we have heard, which we have seen with our eyes, which we have looked upon, and our hands have handled, of the Word of life...That which we have seen and heard declare we unto you, that ye also may have fellowship with us: and truly our fellowship is with the Father, and with his Son Jesus Christ.***

1 JOHN 1:1, 3 (KJV)

The scope of intimacy in discipleship is broader than a mentor-mentee relationship. Discipleship facilitates continuous fellowship with the Master that enables you to look like Him.

However, fellowship with the Master does not stop you from submitting yourself to a mentor or a coach who will train you to acquire certain skills and teach you wisdom in taking critical steps in various aspects of your life.

Although a coaching routine or mentorship training was designed to present to you a certificate on completion of the training, discipleship has no such provision. Our final assessment comes when our Master returns and we behold Him face to face, unashamed, because we will look like Him (1 John 3:2). There is no graduation in view until you grow into His full stature and become as He is. Therefore to follow Jesus is to walk in intimate agreement with Him daily.

Prophet Amos once asked, "Can two walk together except they agree?" (Amos 3:3) The answer to that question is, No! Except a disciple consciously walks in obedience to every command and instruction the Master gives, there will be friction in that relationship.

If you desire to attain the full stature of Christ, intimacy with the Master is essential. Nobody will trust you with their fullness if they do not first have your heart.

Jesus' first disciples had enjoyed close fellowship with Jesus when He was with them. While He taught the multitude with parables publicly, He expounded the parables to His disciples privately. The disciples had access to those mysteries that sounded uncompressible to the multitudes and the Pharisees, because they had an intimate relationship with the Master. You would be a great disciple if you have the platform to engage the Master personally and ask all manner of questions.

The multitudes were familiar with the acts of Jesus, but they did not know His ways. Only the disciples who went beyond the public places to enter into the secret places, where intimacy was cultivated with the Master knew His ways. They will ask Him, "Sir, when you were preaching, you said this, so how is it happening? We do not understand it." This level of access and intimacy creates the pathway to entering the full stature of the Master.

There was one of our disciples who followed me everywhere that he began to observe my carriage and attitudes while travelling for meetings. During one of such journeys, he noticed that I was not doing any visible spiritual exercise. Yet, God opened two blind eyes that evening at the meeting I was invited to preach.

How could this be? He wondered that such a demonstration of power should have been birthed in earnest prayers all through the journey. His curiosity got him an invitation to my closet. He stayed awake all night to watch what I could be doing differently to generate such power. He watched me pray earnestly through the night. That brother got close to know my ways; he did not stop at celebrating the acts like many Christians do today. Do not be like one of those. Desire the ways.

The secret that disciple discovered that day unlocked his potentials to also replicate what he saw me did in another dimension.

You cannot be a disciple who pursues intimacy with the Master without producing greater dimensions of His works on earth.

REVIEW

- The ultimate command of Jesus to His disciples was to make disciples not converts.
- The essence of the disciplines of discipleship is to make disciples conform to the Master – Jesus.
- The disciplines of prayer and fasting generate a lot of power.
- Prayer is to every disciple as oxygen is to

man.

- Through the discipline of fasting, you subdue and deprive the body of pleasure.
- The result of practising the prescribed disciplines is intimacy with the Master.

CHAPTER 5

THE NON-NEGOTIABLE PROOFS OF DISCIPLESHIP

The strength of true discipleship lies in continuity. Dogged commitment in following through on discipleship training would produce certain non-negotiable proofs that every disciple ought to manifest.

Primarily, three non-negotiable proofs must manifest daily in our lives as proofs that we are true disciples of Jesus.

THE PROOF OF CONTINUING IN THE WORD

The first proof that you are truly following Jesus is your appetite for the word of God and your attitude towards it. The gauge Jesus uses to identify His true disciples is not just reading and practising the word occasionally, but commitment to continue in it. It is not so difficult to start reading the word and follow its precepts. Anything could motivate you to start; it could be an inspiring sermon you just heard or a challenge you got from another disciple. But to continue in the word, you will need more than that initial stimulus.

The Christian race is a life race; it is not a hundred or a two hundred meter dash. Once you start, you keep at it your whole life. Many Christians get tired in the process of running because it seems unending. There is an end. The end of this race comes when you stand before the Master and He says to you, "Well done thou good and faithful servant. Enter into the joy of your master (Matthew 25:23)." To arrive at that end, you have to become an ardent follower and practitioner of the Master's word.

Then said Jesus to those Jews which believed on him, if ye continues in my word then are ye my disciples indeed;

JOHN 8:31 (KJV)

Many words are flying around today that looks like the word of God. You can get some from motivational speakers. You can get many words from different sources on the internet too, but they are not the word of God. Jesus emphasised that the evidence that you are His disciple is that you continue in His word not any other word.

With all the options that confront us all daily – options that compel us to make critical decisions, we will need more than motivational speech to make right decisions. The ability to continuously set our hearts to seek instructions and counsels from His word guides our hearts in making decisions that please Him. This also proves our loyalty to Him.

Be determined to continue in His words. Regardless of the other options you have, make up your mind to tenaciously hold on to His word alone. Do not start this race with His word to forsake it later. More so, No excuse is substantial enough to make you drift off. Your decision to continue in the word or not will determine if you will finish strong or not.

Contentions that Comes from Continuing in His Word

Will there be challenges along the way? Definitely! There will be lots of them; they will come in different shades. But you must continue to hold on to God's word with grit. Your Master is the author and the finisher of your faith. This implies that everything that pertains to how you will start and end this journey is in the word of the Master. This is why you have to remain and continue in His words.

There is usually a strong urge from our flesh that suggests to us that we should just quit it all. This urge comes to us daily. It creates a fierce contention within us. Our soul is usually left to contemplate the suggestions from the word and the flesh. However fierce the contention might be, you must know that the flesh does not speak the mind of God. It always says things contrary to what God say (Romans 8:7-8). The mind of God is revealed only through His word. Thus, you must devotedly commit to doing what the His word says.

Instructions from His Word might make you look foolish before natural men. They might call you names when you begin to obey those instructions and continue in it. They might harass you. Do not let any of that change your conviction. Jesus was treated likewise in His days. They even told Him to save Himself since He had been saving others. He was not deterred by any of those, so you must not. The courage to committedly devote to continue in the word of God will make you grounded in your commitment to your conviction.

It Is Not Seasonal

To continue in God's word is to believe and obey the God's word in all seasons of life. There are many Christians who cannot continue once the weather gets rough or when things are not working well for them. They pull back into shells of depression and gloom to be fed with more lies by the devil. A true disciple is to hold on to God's word in season and out of season. That was what reinforced the courage of Gideon, Daniel and the three Hebrew boys. Everything suggested negative outcomes, but persuasion about their convictions and the thrust for continuity in the laws of God kept them going.

Your continuity in God's word will bring you honour at the end.

THE PROOF OF UNQUENCHABLE LOVE FOR OTHERS

The second non-negotiable proof of a disciple is unquenchable love for others. Love is an amazing proof that we are disciples of Jesus.

> ***By this shall all men know that he are my disciples if you have love for one another.***

JOHN 13:35 (KJV)

One of the most misjudged words in human vocabulary is "love". Many singers sing about love, we hear talks here and there about love daily because every sane person believes it is an essential for living together in peace, yet, it is a very scarce commodity in our generation. We talk about it, but we do not demonstrate it. It is easier to say you love someone, but it is difficult to pay the price of love because, in reality, there is no love without a price. Hence, a lot of people can claim to love God, but do not go beyond proclaiming it. We need to go beyond proclamation to demonstration regardless the cost. Love is costly.

Loving one another requires a measure of commitment just as loving Jesus requires a great measure of commitment. At times it is easy for you to say you love God, but the proof that you truly do is what you do to your neighbour. The whole world is currently in a very strange season; chaos in different nations – both advanced and even the third world nations, suspicion deception, betrayal, murder and a lot of vulnerability to attack and all manner of assaults in some unsuspecting corners are the things that characterize the present world. All these make it difficult to love anyone.

If you are asked to share your meal with a neighbour, who you barely know, who has not had anything to eat for days, how will you respond? You do not need to know people to show them love. The Master commanded us to love our neighbours. You need to show love to all groups of people that comes around you because it is a commandment.

Love is a generalized word. There is a type of love that compels you to love someone from your tribe. It makes you relate comfortably with folks from your region or nativity, especially if you speak the same dialect. There is nothing wrong with that. But the love Jesus commanded us to demonstrate is not tribal or denominational. The reason you love only people from your denomination is because you share the same doctrinal practices. Thus, every other person who is not from your denomination is marginalized because they do not practice Christianity the way your church preaches it. That is not the kind of love Jesus commanded.

Loving God and loving one another must be completely detribalized. Do not love people because they are from your clan, tribe, nation, or denomination, rather, demonstrate love to people because the same redemptive blood has drawn us together, and that redemptive blood is stronger than any other blood.

This blood is not a noisy blood that proclaims its love without commensurate service. It does not demonstrate its love for accolades and attention. It is selfless. It is not the kind of love that constructs a playground, donates motorcycles with some bags of rice and goes about publicizing it to the world. The redemptive blood speaks of a better love; love that comes with a lot of sacrifice.

Nobody knew how impactful Dorcas' generosity, propelled by love, was until she died. People showed up from different communities with evidences to testify of Dorcas' love (Acts 9:36-42). Can you love this much?

Our discipleship training will remain questionable until we pass the test of love. As a disciple of Jesus, how many lives have been touched and transformed by your act of love? How many lives have you brought out of nothingness and hopelessness till they arrive at a place of glory, not because you felt obliged to them by any natural factor, but just because of the redemptive blood? What a love!

What kind of love strains his neighbour? It is not borne out of the redemptive blood.

The love that proves a Christian as a true disciple is unquenchable, one that no offence can quench no matter how severe. Assuredly, offences will come, but you must not allow them to quench your love. Your love must be daring and boundless.

No marriage will be under threat if it was built on an unending sacrificial commitment to one another. Replicate the selfless love you demonstrate to your brethren in your home too. Do not just sacrificially love your brethren alone; love your spouse and children sacrificially too. This will make your home survive all seasons of life.

The reason why the first church in the book of Acts of Apostles lacked nothing was not because they were all rich. It was because some brought their money and laid it down at the apostles' feet. Some sold their precious landed properties and brought the proceeds to the apostles' feet (Acts 4:32-35). There was continuous sacrificial giving propelled by love for one another at that time. It was a beautiful time!

At the time when we just started our ministry, we were not many at the time. There were only two sisters with us then. Whenever we come to fellowship together during our Bible Study, everyone gave everything in their pockets as their offering. Those two sisters' offerings were usually the biggest because of their families' financial status. After the offering has been collected, we redistributed it right thereafter the fellowship. At that time, most of us were not buoyant financially, and there was nothing to fall back on. So, whatever we got from that distribution catered for some of our basic needs. It was delightsome. Most times, those two sisters who gave the highest amount of offering may take nothing home than just transport fare to get back home. Nobody complained when we redistributed the offerings. Nobody felt inadequate; the one who gave the most did not appear oppressive to the one who received the benefit; that is love.

We need to return to that basic love life, where caring for another person does not become offensive; it does not become something that we put on the front page of the newspaper. Let your acts of love be known only to your heavenly Father who sees in secret and will also reward you openly. God indeed rewards men. You cannot be stranded if you live your life this way. You cannot be a giver and be stranded. You cannot be praying for other people because you love them and lack prayers for your own life; it is a seed. God rewards men who out of love pray for other people by raising others to pray for them as well.

THE PROOF OF FRUITFULNESS

There is a lot of excitement that comes with the word *fruit*. Anyone that picks up a good, ripe fruit in its season is usually happy. Usually, we get attracted to fruits but pay little or no attention to the processes that produce the fruit. In the context of our discussion, consistent continuity in the word of God and loving one another are processes that guarantee the production of fruits in our lives. Fruitfulness is very important in discipleship.

Fruits are very attractive when ripe. Fruits attract attention when ripe and they attract opposition when ripe. People throw stones at ripe fruits when they cannot get it from their position. Also, fruits are easily noticed from a distance. When your life as a disciple becomes fruitful, people will notice you, but they will also throw stones at you. It is a proof that you are ripe.

Thank God for your born again experience, but without any fruit to show, it is tantamount to failure. Without fruits to show for your years of salvation experience is to have failed the purpose for planting you in Christ. You were called by God to bear fruit.

God is the husbandman; He sowed you to the earth to bring forth fruit. It is not enough to be counting years of conversion; you should be able to count the lives that have come to the kingdom by your efforts. No reason is sufficient to justify the fruitlessness of a believer.

The field of the world is ripe for harvest but the problem has always been the harvesters. The labourers that should enter into this harvest are loitering around. Those who are yet to be harvested are now thorns in the flesh of the church, as they were denied the truth when their heart was still accessible.

Many Christians today are merely living to survive–running the rat race for survival. Being involved in the rat race of survival is a signal of not being a true disciple. In your daily endeavours, you meet sinners on the road, in the bus, in your office, in the market, or anywhere else. If you are passionately committed to bearing fruit, you will not be comfortable just loitering around, scavenging for what to eat.

You do not need one hour or more to share the love of Christ with a sinner who is your colleague. You can do so under a few minutes. It is a seed you are sowing.

People make time for things that are important to them. We all make time for eating because it is a priority to eat, if we do not, we risk having health issues. We all make time to sleep because we need it to help our system. Employees make time to go to work because they need the salary to keep soul and body together. Students make time to go to school because they need the certificate. If we prioritize soul-winning too, we will make time for it as well.

Would it not be a great decision to decide to win a soul every month just the way you receive your salary once a month? You can also decide to preach to at least one sinner every day since you also eat every day. You can choose to do it anyway; in as much you are committed to bearing fruit. God will be pleased with you and He will be glorified too.

The need to Preach the Gospel

People are hurting beyond physical food. Some people are confused spiritually and without any sense of direction. They do not even know where to turn to; you just see them every day, but you have no idea what they are going through.

Recently, somebody told me he had attempted suicide three times. It sounded unbelievable because of his status and wealth. It is an indication that wealth or outward look does not mean all is well. You never can tell, just one minute of engaging one of such persons can avert a suicidal attempt.

In preaching the gospel, do not ever look at anyone and speak from a negative perspective to that person. Rather, look for something good to say about them first, at least to break the silence within them and to gain access to them.

Evangelism is for All

Evangelism is not just a department in a church; it is the mandate of all believers. Once you are saved, stand up for the salvation of other people. Nonetheless, it is good to still have an evangelism department in the church but we must ensure that the department is functional. As a church leader, every member of your church should know that beyond singing, ushering, and giving announcement or any other thing they do in the church, they must also be soul winners. If we all become soul winners we will bring joy to God in heaven because there is joy in heaven over one sinner that repents (Luke 15:7).

God Rewards Fruitfulness

If you keep giving God joy through your acts of obedience in soul winning, it will be unrighteous for God to watch you in pains, crises or confusion without doing anything. If you take this new order, you will find answers to prayers even without praying about them because every true father is excited when his children do what gives him joy. Be a soul winner and the Lord will be there for you.

REVIEW

- Continuity in God's word is a proof that you are a disciple.
- Continuity in His word is not subject to seasons; you must continue in all seasons.
- Love should not be bias but selfless because the Love that purchased us is selfless.
- Through your fruitfulness in soul-winning, you give glory to the Father.

- There is a reward for fruitfulness.

FINALLY...

Know Your Place In Discipleship

Jesus chose very strange characters – people you might consider misfits for ministry - out of the several qualified people. Among the people He called were a waterside boy, a hot and unrefined fisherman, and a refined man who has stolen so much government money. Irrespective of your professional background, there is a space for you in the fold of Jesus. You may be a crook today, but if you turn to the Master, you will get a space. You may be a moral person, refined from birth till now; there is a space for you.

The beauty of such a mixed community of disciples is that they all come with diverse personalities. In such environment, you cannot expect everyone to talk like you, walk like you, reason like you, and be like you in all other things.

Those who do not have the same personality as you were strategically placed there to reshape you. That seemingly cold-hearted brother around you is there to help you just as you are in that same community to help someone else too.

Life can be boring if we all look alike. Life can be boring if we all have the same attitude. Blessed is all the character God has surrounded you with because they are there to sharpen you as you sharpen them too.

The Master intends to bring all kinds of people together. Because of this, there is a continual working of God's grace upon everybody.

Now when John had heard in the prison the works of Christ, he sent two of his disciples

MATTHEW 11:2 (KJV)

As beautiful as diversity is, you must discover yourself too, else, other personalities will define your life for you. That could be chaotic. Also know your place in the entire community. You are not supposed to be everyone doing everything. Your calling will define the type of person you will be and the environment where your assignment will find more expression. You cannot be everywhere.

During his dire moment of need, John the Baptist was aggrieved that no one came to help him out of the prison, not even Jesus, the Lamb of God who He had introduced by the river came to his aid. Jesus' response to John's disciples further infuriated him and he got offended. Jesus' concluding statement revealed what was already going on within John, He said: "...blessed is whosoever shall not be offended in him (Matthew 11:6)"

The challenge and problem here is that because of the circumstances that John found himself, offense was beginning to take place.

John had concluded that Jesus ought to show up and supernaturally intervene to set him free. But it did not happen just that way. John might not have been arrested if he had stayed in the place of his calling. The prophecy about John was that he would be a voice crying from the wilderness, and as long as he was crying from his place of assignment, no power could harass him. While he was crying in the wilderness, custom officers came to meet him, and he told them the truth. Military personnel went to listen to him, even kings. They all went to the services he held in the wilderness. He preached fiery messages at his services without mincing words. He rebuked those who needed to be rebuked and nobody laid a finger on him, as he was a voice that should come from the wilderness.

The day John the Baptist took an invitation to go to the palace, it was the dance of a little girl that cost him his head and his life. This is why you need to know your placement and location and stay there!

Stay and be raised where God placed you. There is always honour for that act of obedience. Stay there and keep raising your voice there until your season of honour comes.

Stay in your Placement

As a true disciple of Jesus, stay in your placement. Are you called to be a worshipper? Do not become a preacher. Are you called to be a preacher? Do not do otherwise. Understand what you are called to do in the house of God and faithfully do it.

Are you called a wife? Live as a wife in your home. Are you called to be a husband? Discharge your duties as a husband. You did not make yourself a man, God made you and now that you are married, you have been asked to be in charge. Take charge of your home. Are you called somebody's child? Be a child that brings honour. Learn to accept what you are called to be. Stay where you are meant to be.

Displacement Leads to Loss of Authority

John lost his authority when he went to the palace. The king dared not confront John's authority when the latter was in the wildernesses of Judea. That is what happens to any disciple who lives his placement. A disciple is without honour once he or she loses his or her sceptre of authority. Do not go to places where God has not called you to. Stay within your jurisdiction, and faithfully discharge your duties there.

Return to God for Restoration

In the day of difficulty, John the Baptist felt should

do something for him, instead of looking back to God.

Do not blame people, but rather, you should build an intimate relationship with the One that called you.

Why?

He gave the instructions.

ACKNOWLEDGEMENT

I am eternally grateful to my Master, the Lord Jesus Christ, who called me out of darkness and taught me to walk on the rugged path of life as his disciple.

Special gratitude to teachers and fathers in the faith, who made their lives bare for me to glean from, and patiently laboured over me; among who are Rev. Dr. Mike Oye, Rev. Yemi Ayodele, Bro. Gbile Akanni, and Pastor E. A. Falade.

I thank my wife, Stellamaris and our four children for their immense support, especially for making our home a conducive environment to learn and express the lessons shared in this book.

Also, I appreciate everyone who has enrolled with our ministry to learn principles of discipleship, and have become living epistles of the lessons shared in this book.

I appreciate the tremendous effort of the editorial team headed by worked diligently to compile this work and ensure it was published at the proposed time.

Thank you all for your inputs.

ABOUT THE AUTHOR

Samson Ajetomobi

REV. SAMSON AJETOMOBI is the President of The Men of Issachar Vision Incorporated (MIV), which commenced in 1989. He is a man called by God with the mandate to reach the unreached at all cost and reawaken the Church to her responsibilities. He is gripped with a great passion for souls in reaching the unreached at all cost. Since the inception of MIV ministry, his strong drive has helped several lives to discover the essence of living for God.

He is much sought after in trainings, conferences, crusades and church revivals across the continents and because of his leadership thrust of over 34 years he is involved with the leadership of several Christian organizations and mission agencies.

He is married to Stella and their marriage is blessed with four young adults.

www.ingramcontent.com/pod-product-compliance
Lightning Source LLC
La Vergne TN
LVHW050321160826
845677LV00014B/3507